LEADING EFFECTIVE MEETINGS

Learn how to lead meetings
that get real results

Written by Florence Schandeler
Translated by Rebecca Neal

Coaching **50MINUTES**.com

EFFECTIVE MEETINGS

- **Issue:** how do I ensure that meetings are not a waste of time and that they lead to real decisions?
- **Uses:** in a professional setting, it is often necessary to hold a meeting to inform, consult or make decisions. It is therefore vital to go about this properly in order to obtain the desired results.
- **FAQs:**
  - Do I really need to plan this meeting?
  - What material should I organise?
  - Who should I invite to my meeting? How many participants should there be?
  - How should I deal with the time factor? How long should my meeting last?
  - What can I do to make sure that everyone participates actively?

In the professional world, all workers are likely to have to lead a meeting at some point. The aim of this guide is to concisely and succinctly answer the questions that commonly arise in this situation.

Passing on information, delivering a training course, consulting partners, voting on changes within the company, etc.: there are plenty of reasons to exchange ideas and collaborate with your colleagues. Several solutions are possible: sending emails, speaking on the phone, talking with each of the people involved, or all getting together around a table to discuss an issue or set a common goal.

Meetings are often seen as the most efficient way of communicating in many cases, such as carrying out training within the company, making a decision or finding out the general opinion. However, because of the way that they bring different participants together, they can soon become time-consuming and turn into a simple discussion if they are not structured to ensure that the group makes progress.

As such, from the preparation to the summary of a meeting, it is essential to give the participants a general framework to make sure that the meeting is effective. This guide will tackle the three main parts of this: the preparation, the meeting itself, and the minutes. We will see how to draw up an agenda and clearly and concisely set out the aims to be achieved, how to best manage communication between participants, and how to follow up to ensure that the decisions made have an impact and to evaluate the actions carried out.

LEADING A MEETING: THE BASICS

THE THREE STAGES OF AN EFFECTIVE MEETING

- preparing and setting objectives
- leading and acting (making decisions)
- ensuring follow-up and communicating the results.

PREPARING FOR THE MEETING

Drawing up an agenda

To avoid simply planning a friendly meet-up between colleagues, it is vital that you prepare for the meeting seriously by drawing up an agenda and establishing the objectives to be reached.

The agenda is a plan for how the meeting is going to work which is sent to colleagues to notify them to attend, preferably in written form in order to avoid potential forgetting or misunderstandings and to provide a formal framework for the meeting. It is sent to all participants before the meeting, but it is best not to do this too early or it might be forgotten. It is generally advised to send it around four days before the date set so that everyone has time to take note of it.

This plan contains practical information: the date, the

start and end time of the meeting, possible information on lunch and other breaks if necessary, the room and the list of people invited. It also includes the list of subjects to be discussed, so that the participants can think about them beforehand and come to the meeting fully informed, which will allow them to get more involved in the discussion.

Setting goals and motivating people

To make the work to be carried out as a group concrete and tangible, you need to formulate clear and precise objectives that all the participants must try to reach at the end of the meeting.

By definition, a goal needs to be:

- Achievable. You should take into account the means and resources that the group has at its disposal and the constraints it faces.
- Measurable. The results that you are trying to obtain must be assessable, and for this reason you must establish clear and precise criteria that will allow you to say whether the goal has been reached or not.

- Useful. For the group to rally around a given goal, they must be able to see what is at stake. A concrete and concise formulation of the objective must highlight the benefits of successfully completing the project.
- Appealing. The goal should create desire in participants so that they actively get together in order to carry it out. Indeed, while the presence of a goal which is seen as shared is an essential condition for a group to recognise itself as a group and decide to act together, it is necessary to keep in mind that this group is by nature comprised of different people who all have their own expectations and opinions. For the different participants to unite around this common goal, dedicating their time and energy and sometimes even sacrificing some personal ideas to it, each person's interests and aspirations must be taken into account.
- Determined by a time factor. It is vital to set a deadline for the carrying out of the task set, as without this it will be impossible to coordinate the activity of all the partici-pants and to maintain the motivation of the group.

Do not try to do too much: it is better to try to reach a single concrete, realistic and measurable goal than to attempt to deal with all the themes directly and have no tangible results at the end of the meeting. Being able to objectively show the participants that progress has been made on the project and that they have not wasted their time with endless discussions is essential to preserve the confidence and motivation of the group.

Identifying each person's role

The existence of a well-established structure which names the group leader or leaders is a necessary condition to ensure cohesion and give each of the participants the freedom to speak and act.

The person running the meeting is the one who takes on the role of leader within the group. They are not to be confused with a person of higher status (like a manager with their employees or a teacher with their students), but rather are granted by the group, in the precise spatiotemporal setting of the meeting, the necessary authority to successfully carry out the activities. They are at the service of the group to facilitate exchanges, clarify the objectives and encourage efficient working.

The meeting leader must first of all remind the participants of the contract which brings them together: the meeting is being held in order to respond to a specific goal that must be reached. They must therefore explain this and ensure that everybody understands. During the meeting, the leader sets the pace: they remain neutral with regard to the discussion, but dismiss ideas that are in conflict with the common aim. Their duty is to ask questions of the participants and structure the discussion. Their interventions in this respect should help the group to progress towards achieving the objective by:

- helping them to coordinate the tasks to be carried out;
- reformulating and clarifying the meaning of contributions;
- bringing together and synthesising the ideas put forward;
- allowing the group to formulate conclusions and make decisions.

The leader is also in charge of setting and maintaining the framework of the meeting. By 'framework', we mean the set of rules which govern and control the exchanges between participants. The leader is therefore in charge of ensuring that rules are observed. One of the first rules is that the meeting does not run over its allotted time: the leader must ensure that this rule is observed and be strict about it. They also ensure that discussion remains relevant to the objectives set.

Finally, it must be remembered that a meeting is above all a time for people to come together, which necessarily means that the participants involved come into contact with one another. The leader must therefore manage this aspect of the groupwork, which is often more complicated than you might imagine. They must ensure that the more reserved participants are not afraid to express themselves in front of their more assertive colleagues and that a tendency towards conformism, where the majority systematically imposes their point of view with no real discussion, does not develop.

To make joint work possible and effective, the leader ensures that exchanges between the participants are respectful and the meeting takes place in the best possible atmosphere. They must take care to make the participants feel welcome and win their trust at the start of the session, by encouraging an initial exchange where everyone can get to know them and the other people present, if they do not already. They adopt a sympathetic and attentive attitude towards the participants, give everyone the opportunity to express themselves, distribute their attention equally to stop anyone from feeling isolated during the conversation, and value every person's contribution.

IN SHORT: THREE KEY ELEMENTS OF THE LEADER'S ROLE

- contract
- framework
- contact.

For the other participants to take an active part in the meeting, they must feel involved in the discussion. By underlining the role of each person in the accomplishment of the objective, the leader reminds them that they have some responsibility for the success or failure of the meeting. It is also possible to predetermine the contribution of some or all of the participants, by explicitly asking them for their opinion when then discussion is dealing with their areas of expertise. For this reason, it is useful to evaluate the possible contribution of each colleague based on their own knowledge and skills.

Another option to increase the participation of some members is to involve them in the running of the meeting, by giving them roles which complement that of the leader.

- The secretary: they note down what is said by the group and summarise in writing the exchanges during the meeting.
- The observer: they observe how the group operates and give their opinion at the end of the meeting on the modes of exchange and respect for the speaking time of each person.
- The timekeeper: they are in charge of ensuring that the timetable is respected.

LEADING THE MEETING

Introducing the meeting

The first five to ten minutes of the meeting are essential, as they set the tone for the work to follow. First of all, the leader establishes contact with the participants by welcoming them, introducing themselves to them and paying attention to them. This step is crucial if you want to foster an atmosphere which encourages exchange. It therefore implicitly answers the following two questions:

- Who am I?
- Who are we?

Then, they remind participants of the theme and the aim of the meeting, which are both set out in the agenda, and in doing so establish a contract with the group with regard to the results they need to achieve together. This step allows the issues that the meeting will deal with to be fixed, so that the participants can gauge its importance and feel involved. It therefore answers the question:

- What are we going to do?

Finally, the leader presents the meeting framework. They explain how and when people can speak and remind participants of the start and end times of the meeting, as well as the breaks which were established beforehand. In this way, they answer the questions:

- How are we going to do it?
- In what timeframe?

Managing communication

Throughout the meeting, the leader manages the different participants' turns at speaking. From their neutral position and caring attitude towards each individual, they get the discussion started, observe the communication and flow of ideas, and ensure that nobody is left out. Their role is to bring out the opinion of the group as a whole in all its complexity. They help to develop the unity of the group, while respecting and ensuring respect for each person's differences. They maintain the framework, call the meeting to order if the discussion is going off topic, ensure that the group progresses towards the accomplishment of their shared goal, and monitor the timing.

The leader must find the most appropriate way of leading the discussion, taking into account the two major difficulties inherent in groupwork:

- the fear of expressing oneself in front of other people;
- the tendency towards conformism.

They establish an attitude of listening within the group and pay attention so that no participants isolate themselves with a private discussion. They intervene in exchanges so as to stop any attempts to limit the speech of participants, while remaining neutral in the discussion.

They can choose to either work with the group as a whole or to divide the team into discussion subgroups of four to six people. In the first case, the leader must see that everyone has a similar amount of time to speak and that everyone expresses their opinion. To do this, it will be useful to have a sheet of paper and note down the keywords of each participant's contribution next to their name. The second case gives the more reserved participants more room to express themselves. The leader then establishes a precise amount of time for the work in subgroups and appoints one person from each table to report back on the ideas resulting from their discussion. They put forward a direct interrogative formulation to deal with the topic as effectively as possible (for example, "Think of solutions to the following propositions...").

As contributions are made, the leader reformulates and summarises the ideas put forward by the participants, thus synthesising them, in front of and with the help of the entire group. This synthesis is carried out on a whiteboard or projector that can be seen by everyone. In this way, everyone can familiarise themselves with the ideas put forward and then select the most constructive ones with regard to the shared objective.

Making decisions

Decision-making is the intrinsic goal of the meeting and signals that the group is taking action and progressing towards the accomplishment of the shared objective. It takes place at the end of a process that can be divided into three stages:

- the entire group puts forward suggested solutions;
- the ideas put forward are put into perspective and analysed;
- the group decides and makes a decision based on the objective set.

Firstly, the leader makes sure that everybody participates in the discussion and suggests possible solutions. Once all these propositions have been reformulated and summarised, the group, which has taken ownership of these suggestions and has had time to familiarise themselves with all of them, can choose the most suitable approach with the aim of meeting the objective.

Depending on the discussion, there are various ways of making decisions:

- unanimity if all the group members share the same decision;
- consensus if the group agrees on a proposal that they think is most suited to achieving the aim;
- majority decision if the majority of the group vote on a decision;
- minority decision if a decision is supported by a minority of participants who have a higher status and therefore greater decision-making ability.

Summarising to close the meeting

At the end of the meeting, the leader establishes an overall summary of the decisions taken by the group. They ensure that these decisions are clear for everybody by formulating them positively and concretely in the form of actions to be carried out. To make the results tangible, they state the actions to be taken so as to respond to the following questions:

- Who does what?
- Where?
- When?
- How?
- Why?

They conclude the exchange by highlighting the progress made by the group and thanking the participants for their contribution.

FOLLOWING UP ON THE MEETING

Evaluating the work done by the group

Evaluating the meeting involves taking stock of how the group worked and identifying areas for improvement in future. Even though this approach may seem a little too pedantic, reflecting on the work done by the group is essential. It allows you to measure the productivity of the meeting and hear the thoughts of the participants, once again emphasising the importance of each person's opinion.

This evaluation can be carried out orally, by setting aside a few minutes at the end of the meeting. The participants are asked to say what they are satisfied and unsatisfied with, and what they think could be improved about the way the group operates. The advantage of asking these questions out loud is that is leads to a discussion between the participants, which could be more spontaneous and sometimes have a greater impact than written feedback. However, asking the participants to respond in writing sometimes enables a greater degree of honesty and objectivity, and can avoid possible tension with regard to feedback on certain dysfunctional elements.

EXTRA INFORMATION

Another possible technique, which can be used to complement initial oral or written feedback, is to ask the participants to write their last word (thank you, challenge, here we go!, etc.) on a Post-it note. In this way, they share their last feeling with the group and the leader can assess the general state of mind at the end of the meeting.

In addition, it is relevant for the leader to also ask themselves some questions about the outcome of their work in order to improve. In particular, they can ask themselves the following questions:

- Has the group made progress towards its objective? Has it made decisions?
- What have I learnt while managing this meeting?
- What did I bring to the group? How have I contributed to reaching the objective?

Communicating the follow-up to the meeting

Whereas spoken words may quickly be forgotten, written words remain. It is therefore important to keep a written record of the discussion and the decisions taken. Two types of document are worth considering to formalise these elements:

- Minutes. These are written with the aim of illustrating the discussion process. They contain concrete informa-

tion about the meeting (date, time, participants), its objective, the problems dealt with, the points of agreement and disagreement, the decisions taken and the problems which remain unresolved.
- Report. This is designed to be a document which goes over the results of the meeting. It contains the conclusions and a series of recommended actions to be carried out in order to meet the objective set.

These documents are produced by a meeting secretary (this can be the leader) who is not involved in the discussion, in order to ensure that the documents remain impartial. The secretary must possess strong listening and analytical skills, allowing them to get straight to the point and distinguish opinions from facts. They work from their notes, any documents that were distributed to the participants, and their observations.

Once this work has been done, you must ensure that the different participants apply the actions decided on by the group in the field.

TOP TIPS

- Prepare for your role as the leader. Preparing for the meeting is an essential step for it to run smoothly. Turning up poorly or insufficiently prepared will be counterproductive for both you and the participants. You should have a thorough grasp of the relevant themes, have prepared suitable material and be sufficiently rested on the big day. Indeed, leading a group is an activity that requires lots of energy and attention.

SOME ADVICE

Everyone has their own way of managing stress. If you cannot disconnect from everything around you, no gentle music calms your anxiety and the technique of picturing everyone in their underwear has never worked for you, you could always try a technique from relaxation therapy: mindful breathing. Close your eyes, place a hand on your stomach and take a deep breath in which pushes your stomach outwards. Hold the air in your lungs for a few seconds and then breathe out as slowly as possible for as long as you can. This exercise allows you to bring your focus back to yourself by making you aware of your body, putting things into perspective and helping you to relax.

- Seat the participants appropriately. You can choose to lay out the tables in different ways. Bringing everyone

together around a big table in the middle is ideal for a long meeting and for a group of no more than 15 people. A round table encourages the exchange of ideas, but it should not be used for meetings with more than six to ten people. Finally, laying out the tables in a U shape is ideal for an informative or educational meeting, where the leader has a lot of information to pass on.
- Start the meeting with some informal exchanges to break the ice, with the help of some group facilitation techniques.

GROUP FACILITATION TECHNIQUES (SUGGESTED BY THE SEDESS EDUCATION ADVISORS IN NAMUR-LUXEMBOURG)

- Morale forecasting
  - Participant's aim: to introduce themselves and be brave enough to speak by sharing a piece of information with the entire group.
  - Leader's aim: to familiarise themselves with the group, to understand the level of motivation of the participants, to know if possible tensions will arise, etc.
  - Instructions: the leader puts forward a series of images taken from the weather forecast (sun, clouds, storms, etc.) and asks the participants to choose the image which matches their state of mind at that moment.

- Crossed presentation
  - Participant's aim: to be brave enough to start

a conversation with a neighbour who they do not know, to be brave enough to speak by sharing information with the entire group.

- ○ Leader's aim: to introduce themselves and establish initial contact with the group, to make group cohesion possible by inviting the participants to talk among themselves.
- ○ Instructions: the leader presents a questionnaire of around 20 questions like those used in the Proust Questionnaire (questionnaire, originally from England, which asks about thoughts, feelings, desires, etc.; made famous by the responses given by the French author Marcel Proust, 1871-1922, in around 1890). The leader then asks the participants to choose, in pairs, three questions that they would like to answer. Each participant listens to their partner's answer (trying, as far as possible, to avoid taking notes on what they say). Finally, the leader asks each person to present their partner, the questions they chose and their partner's responses. They then debrief participants on the activity by asking how they found it and what they learnt from their neighbour.

- Stay firm in your handling of difficult situations. Anyone can experience conflict or a challenging participant. In a hostile situation, call the participants back to order by framing their responses and returning to the established contract: "We are here to reach this goal". If the conflict is between two participants, reframe the discussion by bringing it back to the objective. If a participant resists your interventions, show that you are open to listening while remaining firm with regard to the framework. It might be the case that a participant will not tolerate authority. In this situation, you should remind them that the role of the leader is not to police the group, but rather to allow it to make progress. If tensions are running too high, do not hesitate to give everyone a five-minute break in order to take a much-needed step back and to allow the different parties to calm down and proceed on a different basis.

SOMETHING TO AVOID

As far as possible, ensure a better mood for work by avoiding holding the meeting at times when your colleagues may be less productive, for example right after lunch, when people tend to become drowsy as they digest their food, or at the end of the day on a Friday, when people just want to get home and relax for the weekend.

- Pay attention to your PowerPoint presentation. Although a PowerPoint presentation can be valuable in supporting the discussion, you should apply some important rules for it to be a success. As such, the text presented on the visuals should be as concise as possible. Apart from the slide featuring the plan of the meeting, you should opt for a single theme, a single idea per visual, and no more than six or seven lines of no more than six or seven words each per visual. As far as possible, use diagrams rather than long sentences to support your ideas. In addition, try to adapt your presentation to your audience: the vocabulary you use can be more or less sophisticated and your presentation can be more or less formal. In any context, there is nothing stopping you from adding a touch of humour every now and then to keep people's moods up.

FAQS

DO I REALLY NEED TO PLAN THIS MEETING?

Because it involves bringing together a series of participants in a single room that has been booked and prepared for this purpose, a meeting demands a certain degree of organisation. It takes time away from participants' working hours and therefore generates a cost for the company. Consequently, before organising a meeting you should ask yourself how useful it is, because there are other ways of communicating: emails, videoconferencing or meeting individually with each person involved. A meeting should only be held if it is the most efficient way of meeting the objective. It is therefore essential to ask yourself if you can get the same results without holding a meeting.

WHAT MATERIAL SHOULD I ORGANISE?

After writing up the agenda and sending it to the participants, the leader collects the material they need for the meeting to run smoothly. They draw up a plan to follow, photocopy the documents that they want to give to the participants, reminding them in particular of the aim of the meeting and the topics to cover, prepare a PowerPoint if necessary to display the necessary information for all participants, and find out if there is a projector and/or a whiteboard (with pens) in the room to gather the ideas resulting from the discussion. It is also a good idea for the leader to have a watch or a stopwatch, which they can place in front of them to allow them to properly manage their time.

WHO SHOULD I INVITE TO MY MEETING? HOW MANY PARTICIPANTS SHOULD THERE BE?

It is undeniable that, the greater the number of participants, the harder it is to manage the discussion and the more complicated decision-making becomes. You are advised to only invite those directly affected by the objective. There is no point inviting people who are not motivated by the topic under discussion and who may not commit to it, or people who do not have the necessary skills for this work.

The optimal number of participants for an effective meeting is somewhere between five (as a meeting with fewer people than this more informal and does not require as much preparation) and fifteen. With this number of participants, it is relatively easy to manage turn-taking with regard to speaking, as the leader can quickly identify the talkative and reserved individuals, and the participants generally feel comfortable expressing their opinions. Beyond this number, you will be dealing with a larger group, which it is harder to manage directly. In this case, you should use other techniques, by dividing the participants into small working groups, so that everybody can take part in the discussion.

HOW SHOULD I DEAL WITH THE TIME FACTOR? HOW LONG SHOULD MY MEETING LAST?

The leader must be strict about sticking to the timing of the meeting. This is the first point in their contract with the participants, through the invitation to the meeting, so their credibility is at stake. Moreover, if the meeting is late getting started because some people arrive late and its end time has to be pushed back as a result, it's a safe bet that other participants will have to leave before it finished because they have a train to catch or children to pick up from school. You must therefore scrupulously respect the timing of the meeting. Starting and finishing on time is the first marker of serious and effective work.

However, because there will always be unexpected events and delays in spite of everything, the leader will sometimes have to deal with latecomers. They will need to get them settled in and integrated into the discussion in a considerate way, while noting their late arrival.

The total duration of the meeting depends to a large extent on the scope of the task on the agenda. For a meeting of over two hours, it is recommended to take a fifteen-minute break after an hour and a half or two hours. This moment of relaxation is necessary to maintain the dynamic and productivity of the group. The timing of these breaks, set out beforehand in the planning of the meeting, must be respected.

WHAT CAN I DO TO MAKE SURE THAT EVERYONE PARTICIPATES ACTIVELY?

Before answering this question, we need to make a small clarification: the leader is in no case the only person responsible for the success or failure of the meeting, and they cannot force anybody to work against their will. The level of maturity, which the richness of exchanges depends on, and the morale of the group and its participants are elements that the leader cannot control.

However, they can put a number of measures in place to boost motivation in the face of the task to be carried out:

- by showing, from the very start of the meeting, that achieving the objective set will be useful to everyone;
- by encouraging a good working atmosphere through the managing of material conditions (a spacious and well-ventilated meeting room, necessary material provided, etc.), through an attitude of caring listening, and through the creation of a space where the participants trust one another and can express themselves freely.

DID YOU KNOW?

The psychologist Abraham Maslow (1908-1970) drew up a pyramid representing the hierarchy of needs of human beings. According to his theory, we seek to fulfil five fundamental needs. To satisfy a need situated at the top of the pyramid, the lower needs must have been fulfilled.

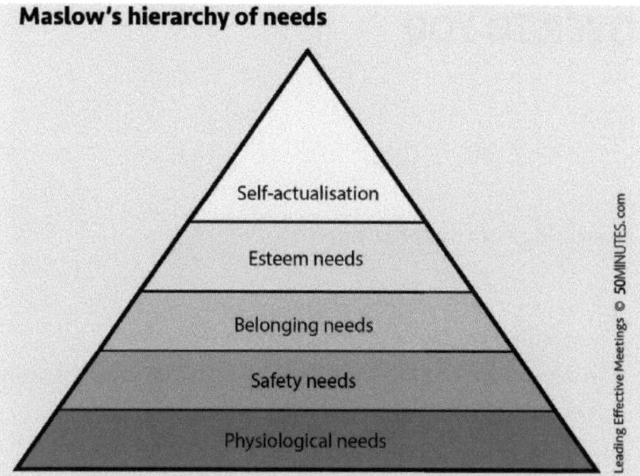

This theory shows us how important it is for the participants to feel comfortable to be able to participate, commit and integrate themselves into the group. In addition, it shows that it is essential to respond to each person's physiological needs – and therefore to take breaks.

OVER TO YOU

TO DO LIST FOR ORGANISING AND CONFIR-MING THE MEETING

1. Preparing for the meeting:

    ◦ establish the agenda;
    ◦ make a list of the participants involved by indicating their contact details;
    ◦ send the agenda to the participants involved;
    ◦ prepare the meeting plan and the files necessary for the running of the meeting;
    ◦ prepare the presentation material;
    ◦ write up and photocopy the documents to be given to participants.

2. Following up on the meeting:

    ◦ write up the minutes/report of the meeting;
    ◦ send out the minutes/report of the meeting to the participants;
    ◦ ensure that the actions decided on during the meeting are carried out by the different participants.

AGENDA: EXAMPLE LAYOUT

Agenda

Date: Time: ___ to ___	List of participants: • • •	Location:
Aim of the meeting: **Topics covered:** • • •		

MEETING PLAN

Meeting plan

Time	Topic	Participants	To clarify	Decicions to take
8:30–8:45	Welcoming participants and reminding them of the agenda.	Leader.	Ensure that everyone understands the agenda. Ask if the participants have any questions.	/
8:45–9:30				
…				

RECORD OF ACTION FOR PARTICIPANTS

Record of action

ACTION	WHO?	HOW? Necessary means	FOR WHEN?

We want to hear from you!
Leave a comment on your online library
and share your favourite books on social media!

FURTHER READING

BIBLIOGRAPHY

- Aubry, J.-M. (2004) *Dynamique des groupes*. Canada: Les Éditions de l'Homme.
- Coqueret, A. (1970) *Comment diriger une réunion*. Paris: Le Centurion.
- Charles, R. and Williame, C. (2010) *La communication orale*. Paris: Nathan.
- Guère, J.-P. and Stern, P. (2002) *Faciliter la communication de groupe*. Paris: Éditions d'Organisation.
- Lainé, S. (2003) *Guide pratique d'entraînement à la conduite de réunion*. Paris: Les Éditions Demos.
- Maccio, C. (2002) *Guide de l'animateur de groupes*. Lyon: Chronique Sociale.
- Mucchielli, R. (2002) *La conduite des réunions*. Issy-les-Moulineaux: Les Éditions ESF.
- Quaranta, M. (2003) *Comment animer un groupe*. Outremont (Quebec): Les Éditions Quebecor.

ADDITIONAL SOURCES

- This guide was produced with the help of SeDESS Namur-Luxembourg.